Go[d, I've Gotta]
Talk to You about
STEALING

Written by Dan Carr
Pictures by Bartholomew and Bill Clark

CONCORDIA PUBLISHING HOUSE • SAINT LOUIS

3 4 5 6 7 8 9 10 11 12   16 15 14 13 12 11 10 09 08 07

Dear God,
You promised that
when I hurt inside
I can talk to You.
I know You love me.
Well, I did something
wrong today. I am sorry.
Today …

I stole a candy bar.

I was shopping with my mother.
We were in the line
where we pay for things.
I picked up a candy bar
and put it in my pocket.

You shall not steal.

Exodus 20:15

I know I was wrong.
My Sunday school teacher
told me what You said.
You said **it is wrong** to steal.
My mom says so too.

In the store I asked Mom
to buy the candy. She said no.
But it looked **so good!**
So I took it anyway.
   I knew it was wrong.

If we have food and clothes,
that should be enough for us.
1 Timothy 6:8 TEV

Then a bad thing happened
to me that was good. My mom saw me.
She was **upset** with me.
She made me put the candy back.
Then I had to tell the store lady
what I did and that I was sorry.
That was not easy.

Before Mom punished me at home, she explained that the candy **belonged** to the store. When I took it without paying for it, I was stealing.

Then Mom told me that
Your Son, Jesus, loves me.
When He died on the cross,
He paid for my sins (like stealing).
She said I should talk to You
and tell You what I did
and that I am sorry.
Jesus, I really am sorry.

If we confess our sins, He will . . .
forgive us our sins. 1 John 1:9

Dear Jesus,

I was wrong when I took something that was not mine. I know I hurt others when I steal. Please, forgive me.

Thank You for dying for my sins. Help my life show that I love You. Amen.